THE DARK HISTORY OF
THE AZTEC EMPIRE

THE DARK HISTORY OF

THE AZTEC EMPIRE

Sean Callery

Marshall Cavendish Benchmark
New York

Published by Marshall Cavendish Benchmark
An imprint of Marshall Cavendish Corporation

Website: www.marshallcavendish.us

Other Marshall Cavendish Offices:
Marshall Cavendish International (Asia) Private Limited, 1 New Industrial Road, Singapore 536196 • Marshall Cavendish International (Thailand) Co Ltd. 253 Asoke, 12th Flr, Sukhumvit 21 Road, Klongtoey Nua, Wattana, Bangkok 10110, Thailand • Marshall Cavendish (Malaysia) Sdn Bhd, Times Subang, Lot 46, Subang Hi-Tech Industrial Park, Batu Tiga, 40000 Shah Alam, Selangor Darul Ehsan, Malaysia

Marshall Cavendish is a trademark of Times Publishing Limited

All websites were available and accurate when this book was sent to press.

Library of Congress Cataloging-in-Publication Data

Callery, Sean.
The dark history of the Aztec Empire / by Sean Callery.
p. c[illegible]—(Dark histories)
Summar[illegible]A collection of dark deeds from the ancient and medieval world"—Provided by publisher.
Includes bibliographical references and index.
ISBN 978-1-60870-085-1
1. Aztecs—Juvenile literature. 2. Mayas—Juvenile literature. 3. Incas—Juvenile literature. I. Title.
F1219.73.C25 2010
972—dc22

2009034700

Editorial and design by
Amber Books Ltd
Bradley's Closelose
74–77 White Lion Street
London N1 9PF
United Kingdom
www.amberbooks.co.uk

Project Editor: Sarah Uttridge
Design: Andrew Easton
Picture Research: Terry Forshaw and Natascha Spargo

PICTURE CREDITS:

FRONT CO[illegible]
Foreground [illegible] (left), mask of Quetzalcoatl, courtesy of Oronoz/Photos 12; foreground image (right), Tholoc, the Aztec god of rain, courtesy of Photos 12/Alamy; background image, El Castillo, Chichen Itza, Mexico, courtesy of Photos.com
BACK COVER
The Spanish destroy Aztec sculptures, 1519, courtesy of Mary Evans Picture Library

Alamy: 34 (Chris Ridley); Art Archive: 11 (Gianni Dagli Orti/National Anthropological Museum, Mexico), 21 (Gianni Dagli Orti/Archaeological & Ethnological Museum, Guatemala City), 41 (Gianni Dagli Orti/Templo Mayor Library, Mexico), 43 (Gianni Dagli Orti/Army Museum, Madrid), 47 (Gianni Dagli Orti/Museo Nacional, Tiahuanacu, Bolivia); Bridgeman Art Library: 3 (Collection of the New York Historical Society), 30 (Bildarchiv Steffens Henri Stierlin), 36 (Bibliotheque Nationale, Paris), 53 (Brooklyn Museum of Art, New York), 54, 57; Corbis: 12 (Werner Forman Archive), 13 (Buddy Mays), 16 (Charles & Josette Lenars), 17 (Gianni Dagli Orti), 22 (Werner Forman Archive), 27 (Bettmann), 33 (Bettmann), 48 (La Venta/Sygma), 50 (Francesco Venturi); De Agostini Picture Library: 10, 24 (A. De Gregorio), 42 (G. Dagli Orti); Dorling Kindersley: 8 (De Agostini Picture Library), 26 (University Museum of Archaeology & Anthropology, Cambridge), 32, 37, 40, 52 (Linda Whitwam); Dreamstime: 2/3 (Jeff Strand) Fotolia: 28 (Grigory Kubatyan), 29 (Palou), 44 (PC Photos), 46 (Alexander); Getty Images: 9 (Bridgeman Art Library), 14 (Manuel Cohen), 18t (National Geographic), 31 (Bridgeman Art Library), 49 (National Geographic); iStockphoto: 23 (Tatiana Murcova); Raymond Ostertag: 6; Photos 12: 19 (Archives du 7eme Art); Photos.com: 18b, 20, 38, 55; Photoshot: 56 (World Illustrated)

Printed in China

Contents

Chapter 1

The Maya

Central Mexico south to the border of Costa Rica in Central America is historically known as **Mesoamerica**. A number of **civilizations** flourished there for thousands of years before the arrival of Christopher Columbus, leading to the Spanish conquest of the region in the fifteenth and sixteenth centuries.

The **Maya** occupied what we now know as southern Mexico, Guatemala, Belize, El Salvador, and western Honduras. The **Aztec** civilization dwelled in what is now central Mexico. The **Incan** society ruled over what is now Peru, Ecuador, and Bolivia.

These early societies spoke different languages and did not know of each other, but each had a dark side. They shared similar beliefs about how shedding blood pleased the gods who they believed created and controlled their world.

This temple at Tikal, in Guatemala, was meant to re-create in stone the mountains where the Maya believed their ancestors went after death.

Mayan Native Americans had a complete writing system of symbols. They were written in books, painted on pottery, and carved in stone.

Mayan Successes

The Mayan culture developed from around 600 BCE and thrived between 250 BCE and 900 CE. No one knows why but, after this time, the Mayan civilization disappeared. While they were flourishing, though, the civilization achieved some astonishing things. The Maya built amazing stepped **pyramids**, and the people also gained a good understanding of the stars and mathematics. And, unlike any other early civilization in the region at that time, they also had a system of writing.

Some of the cities the Maya built were just as heavily populated as many of today's modern capitals.

The Maya was not one single group but about twenty separate **city-states** that seemed to be constantly at war with one another. And underneath this warlike nature was a set of beliefs that prized **sacrifice** and **bloodletting**. In the Mayan world, the blade was the most important tool.

The Gods Have Suffered for Us

The Maya were farmers and their most important crop was maize (corn), a staple in their diet. They wanted this crop to grow well. They believed in a set of gods who could make this happen, including the maize god. The Maya held that the gods had suffered and shed blood in order to give life in the form of crops. The Maya believed that cutting themselves and releasing their own blood was a way of making an offering to the gods in return for allowing their crops to grow abundantly.

Dream of the Gods

Blood was important to the Maya. A person's importance and role in life was decided by bloodline, in other words, the family in which you were born into. So the son of a king would be next in line for the throne. There were two reasons for the importance of bloodletting. One was to offer it to the gods. Another was that losing blood made people feel faint. They hoped to fall into a deep sleep where they might meet the gods or their ancestors (dead relatives) in a dream.

Bloodletting

The Maya had many ways to draw blood. They used sharp items such as stone knives, arrows, or sharpened bones. They also made blades by breaking up the glasslike rock (called **obsidian**), which was abundant in Central America, formed by erupting volcanoes. However, they looked to the sea, too. The pointed spine of a stingray or the sharp tooth of a shark were also used to draw blood. Whatever it was, they pushed the sharp point through soft flesh such as the cheeks, lips, ears, or, most commonly, the tongue. Sometimes they just made cuts to produce a few drops of blood. At other times they would push in a piece of straw so that the wound did not heal and would continue to bleed. At its most extreme, they would pull a length of thin twine through the gap. It might have barbs or thorns in it so pulling it kept the wound bleeding. All of this was to keep up a flow of blood. The blood was splattered onto paper made from the thin bark of a tree. The paper would be

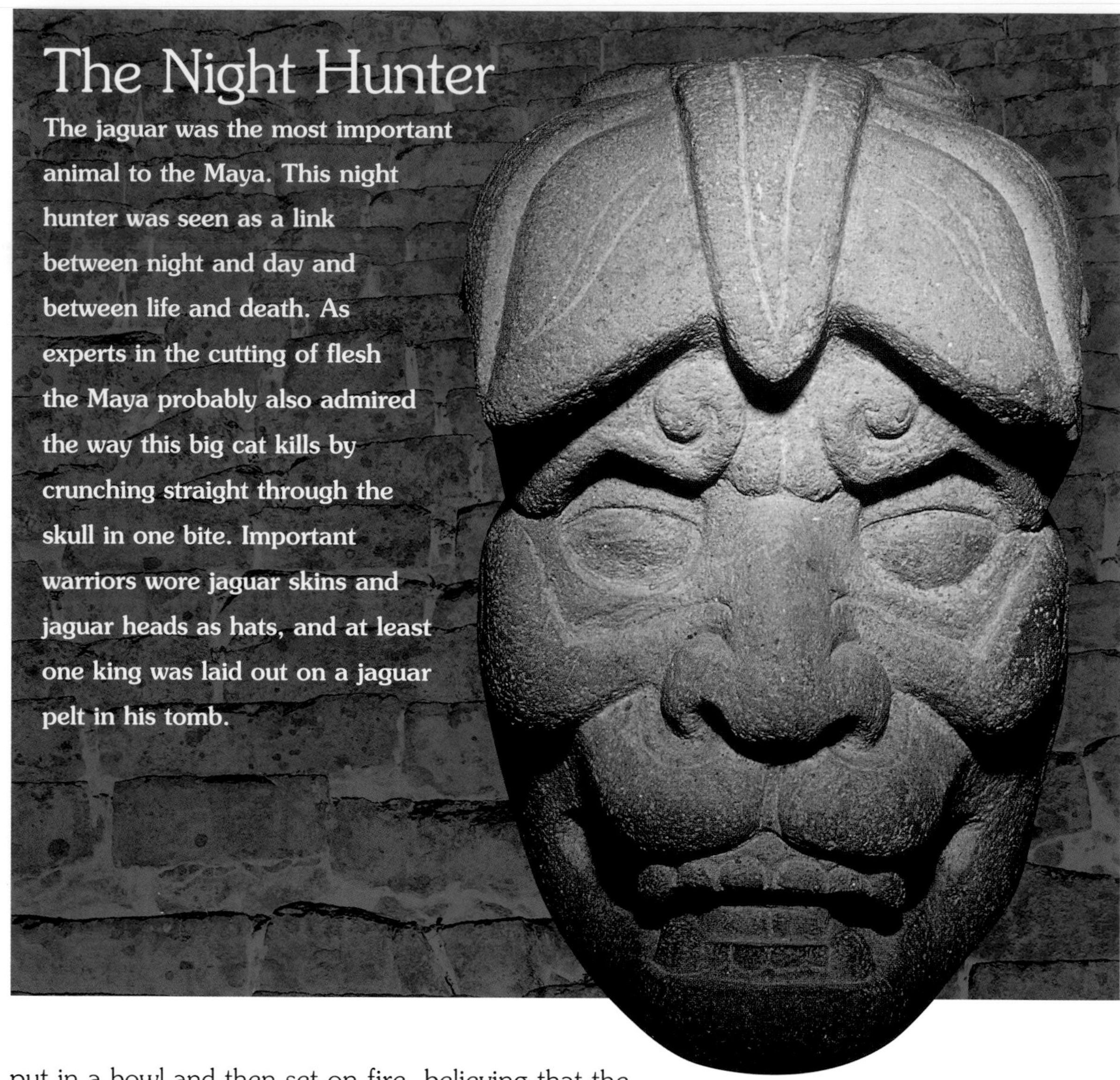

The Night Hunter

The jaguar was the most important animal to the Maya. This night hunter was seen as a link between night and day and between life and death. As experts in the cutting of flesh the Maya probably also admired the way this big cat kills by crunching straight through the skull in one bite. Important warriors wore jaguar skins and jaguar heads as hats, and at least one king was laid out on a jaguar pelt in his tomb.

put in a bowl and then set on fire, believing that the rising smoke carried it to the gods. At other times the blood would be splashed onto statues of the gods.

A Way of Life

This **ritual** was performed at many ceremonies, such as those to celebrate the completion of a new building, or at a marriage or birth. It was also used during burials, or in times of trouble when there was a drought or the ruler was ill. The highest officials, including the king, offered up the bloodletting rituals in public, and the event was recorded in carvings and pictures. It was almost a way of life for some people, and there are reports of some Maya offering their blood to the gods twice a day.

Warlike

Wars were common among the city-states. This might have been partly because, as farmers, they needed more and more land to grow their crops. The easiest way to grow more crops was to take over the lands already cultivated by their neighbors, so there would be wars over boundaries. Another reason for warfare was to prove who was the most powerful.

The two most powerful kingdoms were Tikal and Calakmul. All the kingdoms were warlike, but they formed **alliances** when it was convenient and joined up to attack or defend against other lands. For example Calakmul fought alongside two other kingdoms in a six-year war with Tikal that ended in 562 CE.

The wars didn't seem to have settled differences for very long. For instance Calakmul sent its forces a distance of 150 miles (240 kilometers) to attack the city of Palenque in the years 599, 611, and 654. This was before the days of wheeled carts, so they walked, carrying all their equipment.

The Maya were good farmers, but their soil was not very fertile. It was important for them to conquer new regions for land cultivation.

Soldiers fought in cotton jerkins or loincloths and cloaks. Nobles and important warriors wore jade jewelry and helmets decorated with feathers.

Slow Start

Battles would start with foot soldiers raiding an enemy camp in a silent attack. They would creep up and seize as many men as they could. Their aim was to take captives so that the enemy had fewer soldiers who would fight back.

When that was complete, the battle would be announced with a great noise of drums, whistles, the blowing of seashell or wooden trumpets, and war cries. There would not have been one big battle but a series of smaller-scale fights as individuals or groups of **warriors** hid and leapt out at their opponents. They were armed with spears, darts fired by a throwing device called an **atlatl**, **slingshots** for firing rocks with, and in later times, bows and arrows.

Many of these warriors wore simple jerkins (a short, sleeveless, close-fitting jacket) or loincloths and cloaks, none of which offered much protection in battle. The fighters with better equipment wore feather headdresses in order to appear much taller than they were, and they sometimes hid their eyes with white shell shields that looked like goggles. They would carry a shield and a spear or an atlatl. Some warriors wore the shrunken severed head of a rival ruler either as a necklace or hanging from a belt.

Taken Captive

Some warriors were killed in the fighting, but those taken captive were highly valued. These prisoners of war were kept as **slaves** who had to labor for no pay in the fields. First, though, they might be tortured for information that would be useful to the victors. A favorite method was to tear out a warrior's fingernails, or to crush his fingers. Mayan images of these punishments also show severed heads lying on the ground, probably left as a warning to anyone thinking of trying to escape or refusing to answer questions.

The war ended if the king was captured. However, he and other nobles faced a different fate if they were caught. They would be sacrificed in a special ceremony.

Fields and Quarries

Captured warriors who had been forced into slavery endured long days in the fields farming maize and other crops. They might have helped to build a new pyramid-shaped temple, probably hoping that they would not be the first victims to be sacrificed in it. Prisoners were also forced to work in the quarries using stone chisels because the Maya did not have metal tools. The stone blocks they had carved out would then be carried or pulled on ropes over rolling logs for miles across the rainforest because there were no wheeled carts or beasts trained to pull. Finally, the blocks had to be lifted and set carefully next to the previous block. Being a slave to the Maya was no fun, but it was better than some of the other things that could happen to a prisoner.

Dying in battle meant that you would go to heaven, so Mayan warriors were prepared to fight to the death. Below is a sculpture of Mayan warriors.

Chapter 2

Mayan Games and Sacrifices

When we look into the past we often find things that seem similar to our world. These remind us that ancient people were not so very different than us. So learning that the Maya enjoyed a team ball game brings to mind our love of modern games such as basketball and soccer. But the Mayan ball game had little to do with sporting achievement and plenty to do with supplying blood gifts to the gods.

The Mayan society is also well-known for its practice of human sacrifice—humans would have their lives shortened in order for the gods to look upon their society with favor. It was a grisly end for people seeking a place in the heavenly afterlife.

This is part of the temple at a Mayan ball court. It was probably built with the help of prisoners of war who were also likely to be sacrificed as part of the ritual game.

Game of Death

Prisoners of war were likely to have helped build the courts for an extraordinary Mayan ball game. These ball courts were used for ceremonies and possibly as venues for other sports such as wrestling, but their main purpose was to play Pok-a-tok.

The game took place on a huge playing surface paved with stone. The Great Ball Court at Chichen Itza is 545 feet (166 meters) long and 225 feet (69 m) wide. The pitch was shaped like a huge capital "I," with the boundaries formed by walls 26 feet (8 m) high. These walls were plastered to make them smooth and were brightly painted.

Pok-a-tok was a team game for groups of anywhere between two and eleven players on each side. The ball was solid rubber and measured about 6–8 inches (15–20 centimeters) across, about the size of a human head. It weighed about 9 pounds (4 kilograms), which is about what a human head weighs. Having such a big, heavy object flying around between players was likely to cause an injury if it hit someone or if they landed badly on the stone floor. So they wore protective clothing such as kneepads and thick belts to protect their hips.

The tall stone walls of the ball court were carved with figures such as this player (on the left), decorated in beautiful patterns.

Tough Task

The goal of the game was to pass the rubber ball through one of several giant stone hoops. The hoops were set 23 feet (7 m) above the ground and the players were not allowed to use their feet or hands to move the ball. Instead, they could only move the heavy rubber ball with their head, hips, elbows, and knees.

The game had many special meanings for the Maya. It may have started as a form of, or training for, warfare. But it also seems to have been linked with ideas of the struggle between day and night, and between the gods of the sky and of the **underworld**, so it was part of their religion. There also seem to have been links between the game and fertility rituals to ask the gods to help crops to grow.

The game could last for days because it was so hard to get the heavy ball through the target. There may also have been some sort of scoring system for getting the ball into the opponent's territory. The end of the game was dramatic because it finished with the death of at least one of the players.

There are three possibilities for who was sacrificed, and it is possible that all three occurred at different periods of the Maya era.

- Some Mayan images show the losing captain offering his neck to the victors. He would then be beheaded.

Mayan ball players were competing for more than the glory of winning the game: victory or defeat could decide if they lived or died.

From Animal to Human Sacrifice

Early on in Mayan times, mostly animals were sacrificed, especially turkeys, dogs, squirrels, quail, and iguana. Archaeologists found more than 80,000 animal bones when they went through the contents of twenty-five Mayan trash pits. In the later Mayan period, human sacrifices became more widespread and were not restricted to nobles. Prisoners, slaves, and children were killed, too.

- It is also thought that the entire losing team was sometimes killed and offered up as a sacrifice.
- There is some evidence that the winning team was sacrificed.

For the Maya, being killed in a religious ritual was a great honor and meant they would go to heaven.

It is possible that other victims, such as enemy rulers and prisoners of war, were sacrificed when the game was finished. The most likely method of killing was probably by **beheading**. However, some players were tied up in the shape of a ball and launched down long stone staircases where their tumbling would break their bones. Then they were left to die.

The Sacrifice

Human sacrifice played a big part in Mayan society, people would be killed in order to please the gods. The victim would be

The chacmool was used as a tray where offerings were placed.

painted bright blue and fitted with a special peaked headdress so that he could be seen from far away. He was taken up the steps of a temple to a high platform while dancers moved to rhythmic music played on drums and trumpets. He would be led to a large sacrificial stone, a type of carved table about the size of a bed. Four assistant priests would hold him down. The last thing he saw would be the **chilan** (main priest) advancing toward him holding a large, heavily decorated knife.

Blue was the color of sacrifice for the Maya. Victims were smeared with a special blue dye which was also painted onto the altar where they were to die.

The chilan would cut out the victim's heart, smearing blood over himself and the statues of the gods. Then the corpse was thrown down to a team of temple helpers equipped with sharp knives. They used these to remove its skin, which was then given to the priest to wear as he danced in front of the crowd.

In later times a **chacmool** was placed on the platform. This was a statue of a figure lying down with its hands held over its belly. It was used to hold the heart of the sacrificial victim.

Chichen Itza is a large site in Mexico with many temples. People were sacrificed to the gods there, especially the rain god Chaac.

Another ghoulish piece of decoration was the neat row of poles nearby, each holding the head of an unfortunate person who had been sacrificed. In this ritual the victim died quickly. Death came far more slowly in another ritual of the Maya. As before, the victim was painted blue and fitted with the sacrificial headdress. Then he was tied to a post. The priest would advance with his knife, not to kill but to carve. He would collect blood from the wounds in a bowl and offer it to the gods. Meanwhile warriors would dance around the bound victim, pausing to fire arrows into his body until it sagged lifeless from its stake.

Chaac the Rain God

As a people who relied on the success of their crops for survival, rain was very important to the Maya. Rain was the major source of water for their lands that were far from the sea and where there were few rivers. In times of drought, however, when the rain failed to come, young people were lowered or thrown into a deep well. There they would drown and, it was believed, become the escorts of the rain god, Chaac, who would bring rain. In the city of Chichen Itza, in present-day Mexico, many human remains have been found in a sacred well, which was believed to be a pathway to the underworld. Some have wounds showing they had been killed before their bodies were thrown in. But many were dropped into the deep well alive.

Anyone who actually survived being thrown into the well was seen as a **prophet** who carried messages from the gods and could see into future. In the late twelfth century a man called Hunac Ceel was thrown in. He survived a night in the water and came out to announce his prophesy that he would become the city's ruler. The prediction came true.

Serve the King

Another occasion for sacrifice was the death of a king. A small group of people was chosen to accompany him into the next world. They were killed and buried with the dead monarch. These people often

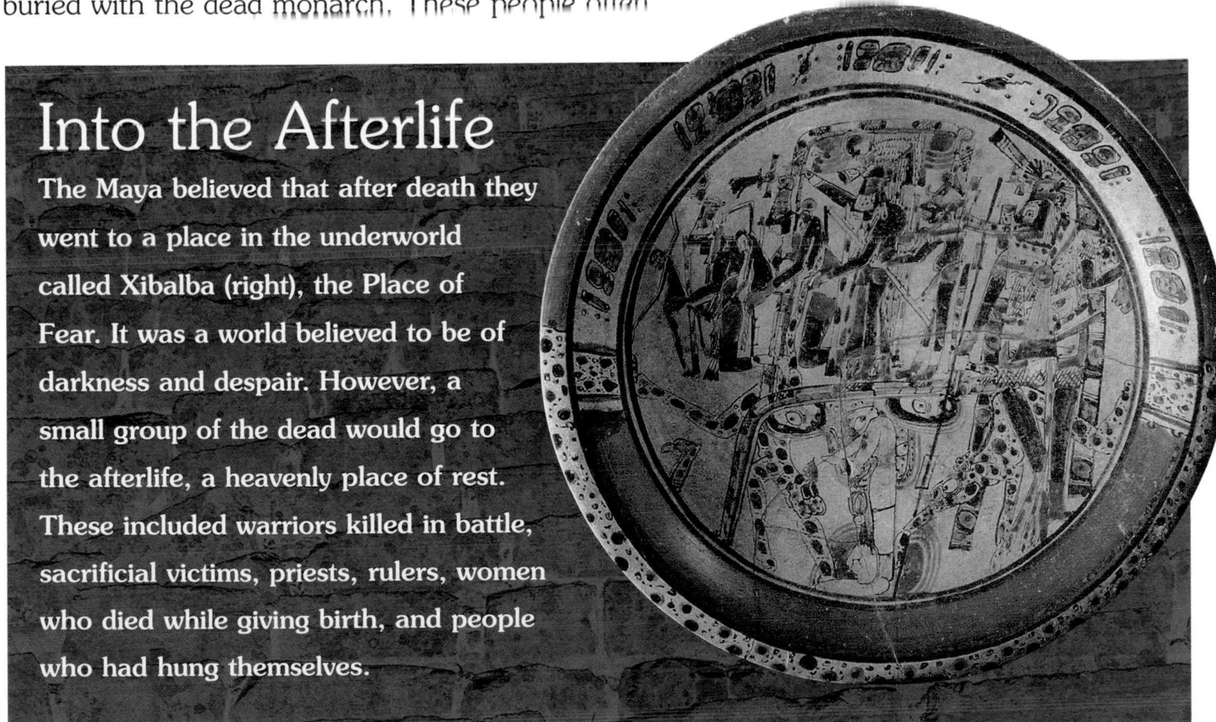

Into the Afterlife

The Maya believed that after death they went to a place in the underworld called Xibalba (right), the Place of Fear. It was a world believed to be of darkness and despair. However, a small group of the dead would go to the afterlife, a heavenly place of rest. These included warriors killed in battle, sacrificial victims, priests, rulers, women who died while giving birth, and people who had hung themselves.

seem to have been quite young, perhaps so that the king would inherit the gift of their youth. They were often royal attendants, and occasionally they were members of the royal family. Their bodies were sometimes richly decorated with jewels.

Sudden Ending

The Mayan civilization went into a sudden and mysterious decline in about 900 CE. By this time the Maya were heavily under the influence of the **Toltecs**, a tribe from Mexico that had begun to invade and take over Maya settlements.

The Toltecs were even keener on human sacrifice than the Maya, who tended to mainly kill opposition rulers and nobles. But the numbers of victims killed in this later period are far higher, possibly contributing to the collapse of the Mayan way of life. Other possible causes include problems in getting food. The lands of the Maya were not very fertile and needed to be left without crops at times to allow the soil to recover. When this didn't happen, the food ran out.

The Maya died out, but some of their beliefs lived on with future Aztec empires.

Tattoos and Teeth

Many Maya had tattoos and body piercings. They would insert large round pieces of jade rock, seashell, or bone through their earlobes or their lips and noses. They also wore necklaces, bracelets, and rings. The Maya would also file their front teeth into different shapes, and often set bright stones such as jade and pyrite into the gaps. A terracotta figure of a Maya warrior with facial tattoos is shown here.

Mayan Beauty

The Maya had strong ideas about beauty and were prepared to do some pretty odd things in the pursuit of looking good. Because they admired long, narrow heads, newborn babies would have boards tied to either side of their skull to squeeze the soft bones to make them longer and thinner. The Maya also liked eyes to be close together, even if it meant becoming cross-eyed. To achieve this look, they would hang a resin ball or a bead in front of the child's eyes to encourage the eye muscles to pull in to focus on the ball, bringing the eyes closer together.

These 15 feet (4.6 m) high warrior statues held up the roof of the Toltec temple at Tula (in Mexico), where many human sacrifices took place.

Chapter 3

The Aztecs

The Aztecs built the largest empire in the history of Mesoamerica. They achieved this very quickly because the Aztec Empire grew out of the Toltec Empire from around the year 1200 to 1520. By that time, the Aztec Empire had a population of 3 million people occupying an area of nearly 125,000 square miles (325 square kilometers) of land across what is now Mexico.

The center of the Aztec civilization was the Valley of Mexico, a huge, oval basin about 7,500 feet (2286 m) above sea level. The Aztec Empire included many cities and towns, especially in the Valley of Mexico. The largest city in the empire was the capital, Tenochtitlan.

This is Huehuetotl, the Aztec god of fire and patron god of kings and warriors. He is often shown as a crouched old man with a bowl of burning incense on his head.

Workers and Killers

The Aztecs were great farmers, warriors, traders, engineers, and artists. They were also some of the biggest mass killers in history with a body count of at least 20,000 victims a year, and possibly even twice that figure. When the Spanish explored one temple they counted 136,000 skulls on display. And these weren't deaths that occurred in the heat of battle. They were sacrifices carried out in carefully managed ceremonies, and it was all done in the name of the gods. In Aztec belief, the gods had to be given human offerings or they would let the universe fall apart.

Sacrifices were carried out on a platform at the top of massive temple pyramids. These structures were covered over with new buildings every fifty-two years. It was as part of the complicated Aztec calendar that called for a sort of rebirth to keep the cycle of life going.

Strict Rules

The Aztecs had very strict rules. For example simple farmers were not allowed to wear cotton because it was considered only to be for important people. The punishment was death. (Typical Aztec dress is shown in the picture here.) You also faced death for chopping down a living tree, moving a boundary marker, and serious theft. Ordinary people were not supposed to drink alcohol (which, like drinking chocolate, was reserved for nobles). If they were found drunk their house would be destroyed and their head shaved.

The Aztecs took human sacrifice to a new level with as many as 20,000 victims killed a year.

Massive Massacre

The most famous sacrifice took place in celebration of the rebuilding of the Great Pyramid of Tenochtitlán in 1487. The Aztecs claimed that they killed 80,000 people in four days. Many people say this figure is unlikely because it would have required killings every few seconds all day and night. It is possible that the Aztec exaggerated the numbers to frighten their enemies and to please the gods. However, even if the scale of the butchering was far lower, it remains an incredible massacre of helpless victims. The line of prisoners waiting to face the knife apparently stretched for 2 miles (3 km).

Animals were sacrificed all the time and were in such demand that the Aztecs bred dogs, eagles, deer, and even jaguar for use in ritual killing.

The Aztec Year

A journey through the Aztec year is a blood-curdling experience. The year was broken down into eighteen months, each lasting twenty days. Each month had its own festival dedicated to a different god, and called for different rituals, numbers of victims, and kinds of killing. Minor gods would be pleased by the sacrifice of a slave. Greater **deities** were only satisfied by the deaths of thousands of nobles or people who had shown great bravery. Young women were drowned for Xilonen, the goddess of maize, while Tezcatlipoca, god of night, was served with the death of only one victim a year. Only children were offered to the rain god Tlaloc. In fact, so many children were often sacrificed that one historian has said that as many as one in five Aztec children died in this way.

The sun god, Tonatiuh, is at the center of the Aztec stone calendar. The symbols of the five world creations surround him.

The first Aztec month began in what is our February and its festival was related to rain. It was celebrated with dances, and by taking children up into the mountains to be sacrificed. The children (often a group of seven) were either slaves or the second born—and so considered less important—children of nobles. They were dressed as the gods Tlaloc or the mountain god Tlaloque and carried up to a shrine at the peak on a stretcher, accompanied by dancing and music. Because their tears were seen as a sign of rain they were encouraged to weep. Sometimes their fingernails were ripped out to make them cry.

Fight to the Death

The next month was when the war was celebrated. There were mock battles and young warriors would present prisoners they had captured in real wars to be sacrificed. This could

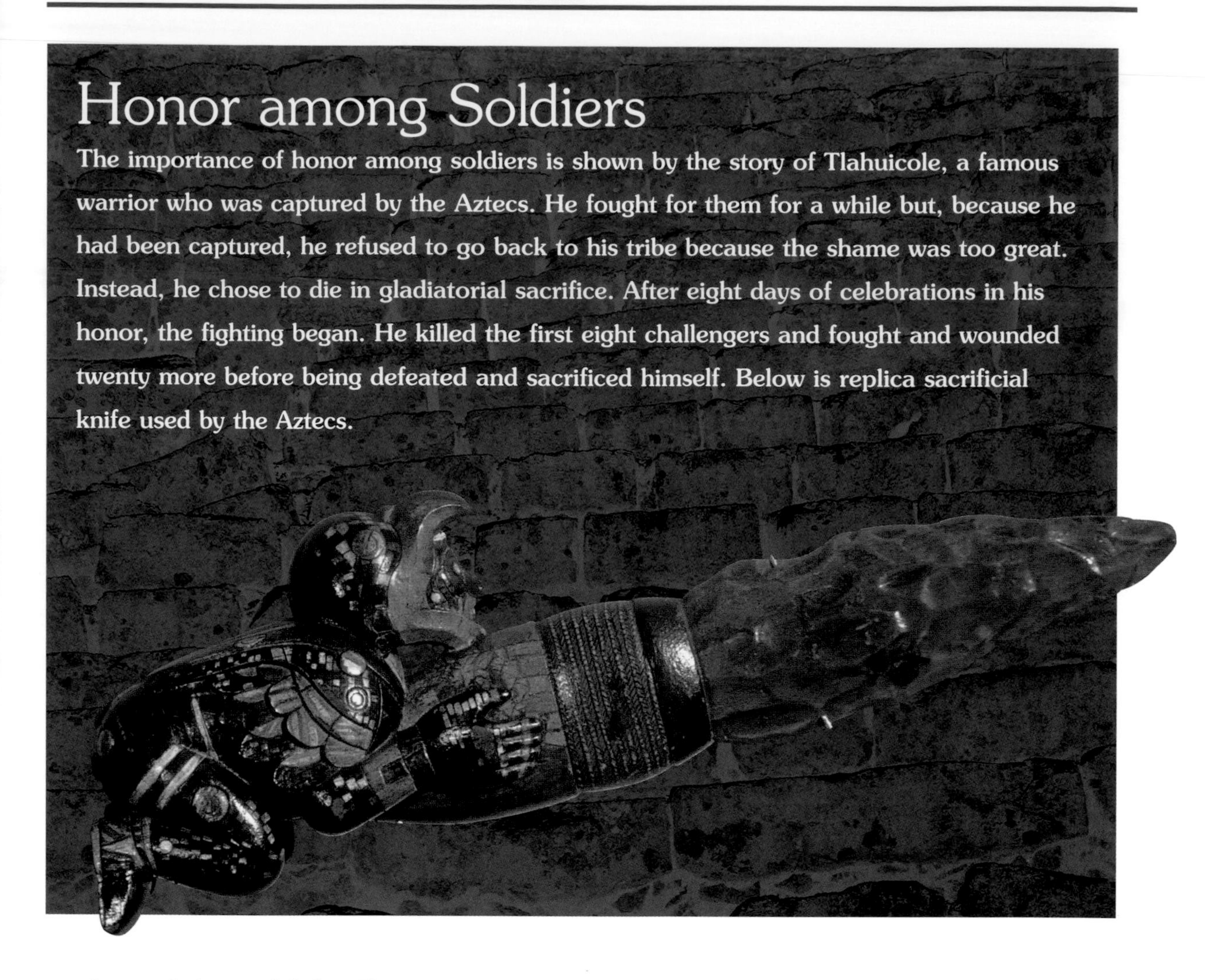

Honor among Soldiers

The importance of honor among soldiers is shown by the story of Tlahuicole, a famous warrior who was captured by the Aztecs. He fought for them for a while but, because he had been captured, he refused to go back to his tribe because the shame was too great. Instead, he chose to die in gladiatorial sacrifice. After eight days of celebrations in his honor, the fighting began. He killed the first eight challengers and fought and wounded twenty more before being defeated and sacrificed himself. Below is replica sacrificial knife used by the Aztecs.

involve a gladiatorial fight. The captive was tied by his ankle to a stone, and given a blunt blade, or one covered with feathers, to fight the heavily armed warriors who approached him. If he did well he could earn his freedom, but the odds were against it.

In this festival the bodies of some victims were skinned after their death and a priest would wear the skin for twenty days. This was an ancient farming **rite** representing the idea of renewal, and whoever wore the skin was looked upon as a god.

More Children

The next festival took place from late March into April. It involved a procession of girls carrying seed corn and flowers to be blessed by the maize god. However, more children were sacrificed, again to encourage the rain. Meanwhile the priest took the skins of the last month's victims and buried them in a sacred cave, the temple of the Xipe Totec. In a separate ceremony, snakes were roasted, offered to the gods, and then eaten.

Aztec rituals were dramatic performances where singers and musicians set the tone. New songs were written and performed to celebrate great victories.

God for a Year

The first occasion in the year when a god was "renewed" took place during the festival known as the Great Vigil. A young man would be dressed up as the god Tezcatlipoca. He would live a life of luxury, accompanied by four beautiful girls. His only job was to play a wooden flute in the streets.

However, this comfortable and easy life would only last a year. Then the "god" climbed the steps of the temple pyramid, broke his flute, and lay down on the stone slab so that the priest could kill him. There were many other similar festivals where people were given the honor of acting as gods or goddesses for a year before being sacrificed. It was an enormous honor and ensured that the person would spend the **afterlife** in heaven.

The Importance of Birds

Birds were important to the Aztecs because they believed the gods could turn themselves into flying animals. In the festival of Acolmiztli, dancing children were decorated to look like birds by pasting brightly colored feathers onto their chests. Birds were featured in other festivals, too. In one festival, the Aztecs tied birds to a pole and carried it while the trapped creatures flew around on strings. In another, birds were sacrificed by chopping off their heads and throwing their still fluttering bodies to the gods.

Climbing the Pole

The ninth Aztec month saw a strange bloodletting ceremony that was a test of fitness and determination. A corn husk figure was placed on the top of a pole made from a thick tree trunk. A group of contestants raced to be the first to climb the pole and cut off the head of the figure. This earned them the honor of visiting a group of elders who would cut their ears with a flint knife to release blood for the gods.

The next month celebrated the fire god Huehueteotl. His human offerings were drugged, probably with herbs or an alcoholic drink, and thrown onto a fire burning on the sacrificial platform. However, before they died they were dragged out with hooks and their hearts were pulled out. In another ceremony involving fire, the victim was sacrificed in the usual way (removing the heart) but then a fire was lit on his chest.

In the following two Aztec months, prisoners of war were sacrificed. The goal of an Aztec soldier was not to kill, but to capture victims for sacrifice. The braver the warrior they brought back, the more valuable he was to the gods and the greater the honor awarded

Children were punished by being held over a fire of burning chilies so that they breathed in the stinging smoke.

to his captor. In the festival, captives were tied up, with their hands and feet bound together, before being killed.

Prisoners kept on for the next festival knew not only that they were to die, but that they would be eaten, too. First, their still-beating heart would be held aloft to the gods. Then their bodies would be returned to the warrior who had captured them.

The body was cut up. The honored warrior could choose whether to give some of it to noble people or take it home to eat. The flesh was cooked in a stew with chilies and tomatoes. By doing this, the warrior raised his own status, making him more important in Aztec society.

At least three of the limbs were the property of the captor if he had taken the prisoner single-handedly in battle. In fact, historians believe that only warriors who had captured someone without assistance were allowed to eat human flesh. Clearly it would have been far easier for a group of soldiers to work together to catch one prisoner at a time, but this brought less honor and status. In the city of Tenochtitlán the other parts of the body, such as the torso, were taken to the royal zoo to be fed to the animals kept there.

Torture for Blood

One Aztec method of torture, possibly linked to bloodletting, was to place naturally sharp things, such as prickly pears, cactus spikes, and the needlelike thorns of the maguey plant on the ground under a layer of straw. Victims would have their hands tied to prevent them from breaking their fall and were thrown onto the straw so that the sharp points cut into their skin.

The most common form of sacrifice was cutting out the heart. This was seen as the most precious thing that could be given to the gods.

The Aztec wall of skulls was a stone version of the wooden racks where the heads of sacrificial victims were displayed.

Cannibalism

There is much debate among historians about how much **cannibalism** (eating of human flesh by people) the Aztecs actually committed. Some suggest that eating dead enemies was a ritual at certain festivals and not something that happened all the time. Others suggest that the vast majority of sacrificial victims were eaten. They point out that some victims were killed and eaten on the battlefield, while others were brought back to the city and kept in cages to be fattened up before the ceremony. Here a victim has been sacrificed to the Sun god and his body lies in pieces on the steps.

Dawn Walk

Sacrificial victims were in no doubt about their fate, because the ceremony had clear rituals. First, they were washed. They were sometimes painted with the color of the festival god. Those being sacrificed to the sun were painted white and wore a black mask to signify the night sky.

As the sun rose they were led along a path strewn with flowers to the sacrificial stone and laid on it. All around them would be music from drums, flutes, and trumpet shells while dancers in exotic clothing, sometimes wearing masks, would perform. The arms and legs of the victim would be held straight, and the priest would lean down to cut below the rib cage then reach in to pull out the heart, raising it, still beating, to show it to the gods.

It seems likely that many were drugged, either with alcohol or some mixture of rainforest leaves that induced dreaming, to stop them from struggling. Those who showed fear as they reached the point of death were jeered at by the crowd and quickly pulled aside and killed, probably by slitting their throats.

Willing Victims

But there seems to have been such a sense of occasion and honor about sacrifice. There were times when victims who could have been saved by Spanish troops insisted that they

Priests

Priests were very important. They served a particular god and lived in the temple most of the time. They were called to prayers three times during the day and once in the night. They were expected to give their blood to the gods, piercing their soft flesh with bone needles or thorns from a plant. They were expected to fast (not eat) for some festivals, and each had a job to do at a sacrifice, such as keeping the fire going, holding down a victim, or, most importantly, removing the victim's heart. Priests would be covered with blood during festivals, and Spanish visitors reported meeting a group of priests whose hair was matted with blood.

The god of death Mictlantecuhtli was honored in rituals that often included the eating of human flesh.

wanted to go ahead and die in this way. Of course they believed they would go to heaven, and maybe they enjoyed being the center of attention in front of a huge crowd. But they would also have understood that blood sacrifice was at the heart of their belief about how the world existed—dying was their duty.

An Unexpected Gift

Two tribes wanted to form an alliance. One of them asked for a chieftain called Achitometl to give his beautiful daughter to join their noble ranks. Achitometl agreed to this great honor and she was handed over. They thought she was to be made a queen. At the end of his visit he was invited to the festivities to celebrate the trip. He saw a priest. He was dancing. He was wearing a cloak of skin. It was the skin of Achitometl's own daughter, which he probably recognized from the tattoos on her body. She had been sacrificed and flayed. The party ended with the angry firing of spears and arrows. The tribes were enemies again.

Tributes

The Aztecs used sacrifice as a way of controlling territories. The Aztec Empire was dominated by three city-states: Tenochtitlán and Texcoco (the two strongest powers) and Tlacopan. Even though outnumbered by other tribes, they controlled a wide territory that spanned from coast to coast.

Conquered towns would agree to pay a **tribute** (like a tax), which could include food, goods, and people. If they could not or did not want to find enough people to send, they would raid their neighbors and steal some of their people to use as tribute. So the Aztecs were able to control a huge empire because the smaller states were fighting one another rather than joining forces and battling against their main oppressor. This lack of overall unity helped the Spanish conquer them, because the invaders from the West were able to play one state off against another instead of fighting them all at the same time.

Slaves to the Altar

Trading was vital to the Aztecs. Merchants traveled long distances to barter for goods. Some of the merchants specialized in buying and selling people as slaves.

People were made slaves as a punishment for committing crimes, but they could still marry and their children were born free. It seems some people had to sell themselves into slavery to pay off money they lost in a gambling game. A slave who had been punished

Flower War

The flower war is the term given to a never-ending battle between states within the Aztec Empire. It apparently began when victims were needed for blood sacrifices to the gods to end a famine. It seems that at the time there was a constant state of war in which the goal was capturing rather than killing enemy warriors. However, it may actually have been a long-drawn out war in which the Aztecs were trying to wear down the resistance of Tlaxcala.

Aztec merchants traveled far from their cities to trade for goods, including slaves.

three times could then be sold, and if that happened three times they could then be used for sacrifice. So it was those who did not please their masters who died.

To celebrate growth and rebirth animals were sacrificed in a fire and children were pulled by the neck to make them grow. Every four years their ears were pierced at the final festival of the calendar.

Chalk or Earth?

Eating dirt was an important part of Aztec culture. It was the custom when you arrived somewhere new to push your finger into some earth and eat it. This was also a sign of honesty: people would say, "If what you say is true, eat earth." During some festivals people would engage in a ritual game where they would eat a mouthful of chalk and then

Live Food

Every eight years on a day known as Tecpatl a special festival was held during which live animals were eaten. A bowl full of water and brimming with frogs and water snakes was presented to the crowd. The bravest (or most foolhardy) would grab a squirming creature and pop it into his mouth to eat. It seems to have been a sort of competition because those who swallowed a snake were given a reward.

Life Force

Blood was central to the Aztec view of the world. Their earth goddess Coatlicue was, according to **legend**, sacrificed as part of the creation of the world. Images of her have two serpents rising from her severed neck, representing the flow of blood. A statue of her is seen here. When the Spanish first met the Aztecs they saw for themselves how important blood was to the tribe. The Aztecs invited them to a feast and set up tables of special food. The Spanish visitors were horrified to see human blood being carefully splattered across the plates as a special extra sauce on their food to show the importance of the occasion.

run as fast as they could through a crowd of people throwing chalk rocks at them.

The Spaniard Hernán Cortés defeated the Aztec Empire between 1519 and 1521. When the Spanish arrived, they were shocked by the sacrifices they witnessed. There is a chilling account by Bernal Diaz of how he and his fellow Spaniards had to watch sixty-one fellow soldiers captured and sacrificed.

He describes a terrifying sound of drums, horns, and trumpets at the start of the ceremony. He speaks of seeing his comrades who had been captured being dragged up the steps of a tall temple. Then the victims had feathered hats put on their heads and were made to dance in front of a statue of an Aztec god. Then after they had danced the priests laid them down on their backs on some narrow stones of sacrifice and, cutting open their chests, drew out their hearts. The bloody hearts were then offered to the gods.

The Aztec people were so amazed by Hernán Cortés's impressive weapons and his horse that they believed he was a god.

Chapter 5

The Inca

The Inca Empire lasted about one hundred years. During all of this time there were wars as its rulers sought to get more land and struggled to control the people they had conquered. It was a remarkable achievement, because a tribe of about 100,000 managed to control the lives of ten million people. Just as the Spanish believed in their right to rule, so the Inca regarded themselves as the most highly developed people in the world with a destiny to rule over their inferior neighbors.

The Inca worshipped their ancestors by burying them in groups inside tall towers like this one.

Triumph of the Few

The Inca was one of many tribes from the Andes Mountains of Peru in the 1100s. In the thirteenth century, under their ruler Manco Qapac and his successors, the kingdom of Cuzco conquered its neighbors one after the other. By the 1400s their empire stretched for 2,500 miles (4,25 km) along the Andes Mountains from modern-day Ecuador through Peru to Chile.

Terraces and Roads

The Inca were good at managing the land. The steep hills of Peru were hard to farm, so they cut them into a series of steps called terraces so that crops could be grown, and set

The city of Machu Picchu had a ceremonial square, temples, burial caves, army barracks, a prison, and a palace for visiting royalty.

Ready for War

Every Incan man had to take part in at least one war in his lifetime. They carried helmets made of wood, cane, or animal skin, round shields made of cotton to cushion blows, and armor to protect against darts and arrows. Their weapons were adapted from hunting. They fought with bronze- or bone-tipped spears, heavy wooden swords with blades with sharp, tooth-like notches, clubs with stone or metal heads, stone or copper-headed axes, and slings to fire rocks.

up a network of canals to supply water. Their engineers also built roads and bridges including one route that stretched 3,250 miles (5,230 km) through the highlands and another along 2,520 miles (4,055 km) of the coast. This allowed their army to move quickly around the empire. The roads also allowed good communication as runners would race along them and hand over their message to a fresh runner. Using this method, messages could travel 150 miles (240 km) in a day.

Trophy Heads

Unlike the Aztecs, the Inca were less concerned about taking captives and were much more likely to kill in battle, and then take body parts from their victims, such as ears and teeth. A common practice was to cut off the head. A hole was cut into the skull and it was hung from the belt as a trophy. They dried the skin and tied the lips together with thorns. Sometimes they shrunk the heads by first emptying the brain through the base of the skull. Then they poured in hot sand, which was replaced every few hours. The heat from the hot sand would shrink the bones so that the head could be worn more easily.

This skull shows the results of trepanation. The Inca believed that evil spirits left through the hole.

The Inca recognized that the head was a crucial part of the body. Many skulls have been found with holes drilled or scraped in the top. This was performed by using a method called **trepanation**. Among ancient peoples, trepanation was a commonly known way of reducing pressure on the brain but it caused headaches and long-term damage. The Inca believed that evil spirits would leave through the hole in the skull, and sometimes they fitted a silver plate to cover it up.

Divide and Rule

When they took over new land, the Inca had a simple yet clever way of stopping people from fighting back in the future. They divided them up and sent them far away to live in other parts of the Incan Empire. This split up the defeated tribe so that they could not organize another rebellion. This way, everyone became part of the Incan Empire.

Death Cult

The Inca thought about death a lot. They believed that the dead went on a journey through the underworld and that they needed those still living to help them. So when an honored person died the Inca would put maize in its mouth (as a symbol of new life and to feed the body as it traveled), along with a bead of jade or stone to act as money to pay for the journey. The body was painted red, the color of death, and was given a bone whistle to help

Getting the Blame

Incan rulers were treated like gods but got the blame if things went wrong. In around 1400 a terrible flood followed by drought stopped the crops from growing. The people blamed their ruler, Fempellec, and seized him. His hands and feet were tied together and he was thrown into the sea to drown helplessly. He was the last ruler from his family.

The Decapitator

Cutting off the head (decapitation) was an important Incan ritual and they even had a decapitator god. He is pictured with a curved knife in his left hand and a severed head in the other. He is sometimes portrayed as half-man and half-spider and at others as half-jaguar. He always sports a terrible set of fangs for teeth.

it find its way. It was wrapped in cotton and buried either in sacred caves, or sometimes under a temple floor. In the cold, thin air, such bodies can be preserved for thousands of years.

It was thought that the spirit of the body only came out after the skin and the flesh had dried or rotted away. Mummies were brought out during religious ceremonies during the year after burial. They were prayed to and offered food and drink. Exactly twelve months later, four young boys would be painted black and would carry out a mock battle as part of a ceremony to mark the end of the journey of the dead person.

Buried Alive

The more important the person had been, the greater the ritual that went with their death. Important people were buried with their wives and some of their servants, all of whom were strangled as part of the burial ceremony. Some were made drunk with an alcoholic drink so that they fell asleep or at least couldn't think properly. Then the tomb was bricked up and they were buried alive in its deep darkness.

Even royal babies would be buried with sacrificed victims. The victim's joints would be broken so their arms and legs would fit into the tiny grave alongside the little royal body. Dead rulers were buried with many more bodies. In the city of Chan Chan a tomb has been found with the corpses of two hundred women who were sacrificed to join a dead king from the Chimu tribe.

Chapter 6

Fighting to the End

The Inca were not alone in their faith in the value of human sacrifice, but they took the idea to the extreme. They believed that in order to please the gods, they should sacrifice their most valued people. They made the ultimate sacrifice—their children.

The Intihuatana Stone at Machu Picchu measures the movement of the Sun to find the twice-yearly equinox, when day and night are the same length. The Inca held special ceremonies on these days.

Child Killers

One of the most shockingly dark facts about Incan sacrifices, either in funerals or other ceremonies, is that they seem to have preferred to kill children. This was because they considered children to be more pure and innocent than adults. The Inca believed the gods were all powerful. It was the gods that made the sun shine, the rains come, and the crops grow, so the human offerings to them had to be of precious, valued people. And what could be more precious or valuable than your own child?

The process was planned well in advance. A year before the sacrifice, the children were

Adults and children were killed at a sacrificial stone like this to become offerings to the gods.

Gory Cliff

It wasn't just children who were sacrificed. Captives were beheaded in religious ceremonies, and one site known as Huaca de la Luna (Temple of the Moon), in northern Peru has gruesome evidence of mass sacrifice. Here the remains of forty males aged between five and thirty were found. They had been pushed off a cliff. They might have been killed first, or it could have been the fall that finished them off. Some had signs of their bones being cut.

selected and given the best food available. They came off their normal diet of potatoes and were fed maize and llama meat instead. This was to build up their strength to survive the months-long march and climb to the mountain where they were to be sacrificed. The Inca believed that high places were nearer to the gods. More than a hundred sacrificial sites have been found above the height of 15,000 feet (4,572 meters) in the Andes Mountains.

New Ruler, New Sacrifice

The death of an emperor meant the start of a new reign. This, too, was marked with sacrifices. Sometimes parts of the bodies were then put in the tomb, probably as proof of the ceremony. Tombs have been found with the bones of hands and feet cut from the corpses of the victims.

Around 1527 when the emperor Huayna Capac died, there were sacrifices for his funeral and to celebrate the appointment of a new ruler. But there was a problem. Capac had about fifty children through his many wives. His eldest son, Hinan Cuyochi should have inherited the throne, but he had died of the same mysterious disease as his father a few days previously.

Huayna Capac was a warrior king who thought he could prevent his sons fighting by dividing his kingdom between them. It didn't work.

Huascar is shown being carried to a ceremony. The Inca believed their rulers were descended from the sun god Inti.

Smallpox

The disease that killed Huayna Capac and his son was smallpox. This was a terrible virus that caused blisters all over the body and affected the vital organs and immune system, eventually leading to death through heart failure or loss of fluid in the body. It was unknown in South America until the arrival of the Spanish and the people had no resistance to it.

The disease killed more people than the Spaniard's guns and cannons, and helped the Spanish conquer the Aztecs and then the Incas.

Two Brothers

Now there was a battle for power between two other sons. The next in line for the throne was Huascar. He was hungry for power and had in fact been plotting to take over from Hinan before his elder brother died. Huascar trusted no one, especially his brothers. While he was alive, the emperor Huayna had shown that he liked another of his sons more. This favorite son, Atahualpa, was given the northern lands where he was popular and had a large army. To his disgust, Huascar was only given the capital city of Cuzco.

Atahualpa seems to have accepted the situation and sent a message offering Huascar his loyalty. Huascar had his brother's messengers killed and sent a set of women's clothing to Atahualpa as a deliberate insult. The brothers went to war. Huascar took the first step. He led a surprise attack to the north and captured Atahualpa. This should have guaranteed them victory. But while the soldiers ate and drank to celebrate their success, a woman slipped into Atahualpa's room with a hidden copper bar. He used this to make a hole in the wall and escaped to reach his army again.

A Human Drum and Cup

A series of battles between the two forces followed. At one, Atahualpa's army captured an enemy general (and another brother to both rulers), Atoc, in a bloody battle in which it is believed that 16,000 soldiers died. Atahualpa's men tied Atoc to a post and tortured him by firing darts and arrows at his body before finally finishing him off. His skin was flayed and used as the skin of a drum. Atahualpa had his enemy's skull gilded in gold and used it as a drinking cup.

There were many more massive battles involving thousands of soldiers before the civil war ended in 1532 when Atahualpa captured Huascar and put him in jail, killing the rest of his brother's family. Now only he could be king. But he had little time to celebrate: the Spanish were coming.

Atahualpa was captured by the Spanish. They kept him inprisoned despite the payment of a huge gold ransom.

The Massacre of Cajamarca

Pizarro's tiny army of a few hundred soldiers reached the city of Cajamarca on November 15, 1532. Atahualpa didn't think such a small force was a threat and he marched into the courtyard with six thousand of his men, none of them armed. But these European invaders came with the darkest of beliefs: that they were superior to their opponents and had the right to do as they wished.

When it became clear that Atahualpa was not prepared to surrender, the Spanish blasted a cannon into the crowd and started firing their guns. The Inca were awed by the noise and the power of these weapons. They had no weapons and no wish to fight once Atahualpa's twelve guards were killed and the emperor was seized and taken to a room in the temple. But the Spanish carried on firing on the trapped Inca before their horsemen charged in swinging their sharp metal swords. In half a n hour, thousands of Inca were butchered.

Gold and Treachery

Atahualpa agreed to find a massive ransom in gold and silver to pay to be released. But he was worried that his brother would make a deal with the Spanish and take over the throne.

Atahualpa lies dead. The priest standing over him had baptized the Inca king as a Christian so that he could avoid being burned at the stake.

Emperor Atahualpa watches helpless from above the battle as Pizarro's men set upon the terrified crowd in the massacre of Cajamarca.

So he had Huascar murdered. This was just the excuse the Spanish needed to get rid of him and they sentenced Atahualpa to be burned at the stake. To the Inca, such a death would mean that they would not reach the Afterlife, so Atahualpa agreed to be baptized as a Christian so that he would instead be strangled. He was choked to death on July 26, 1533, when a metal band was fixed round his neck and tightened until he suffocated.

It was the end of the Incan Empire.

United States
Mexico
ATLANTIC OCEAN
PACIFIC OCEAN
SOUTH AMERICA
Peru
Brazil
Chile
The Mayan Empire
The Aztec Empire
The Incan Empire

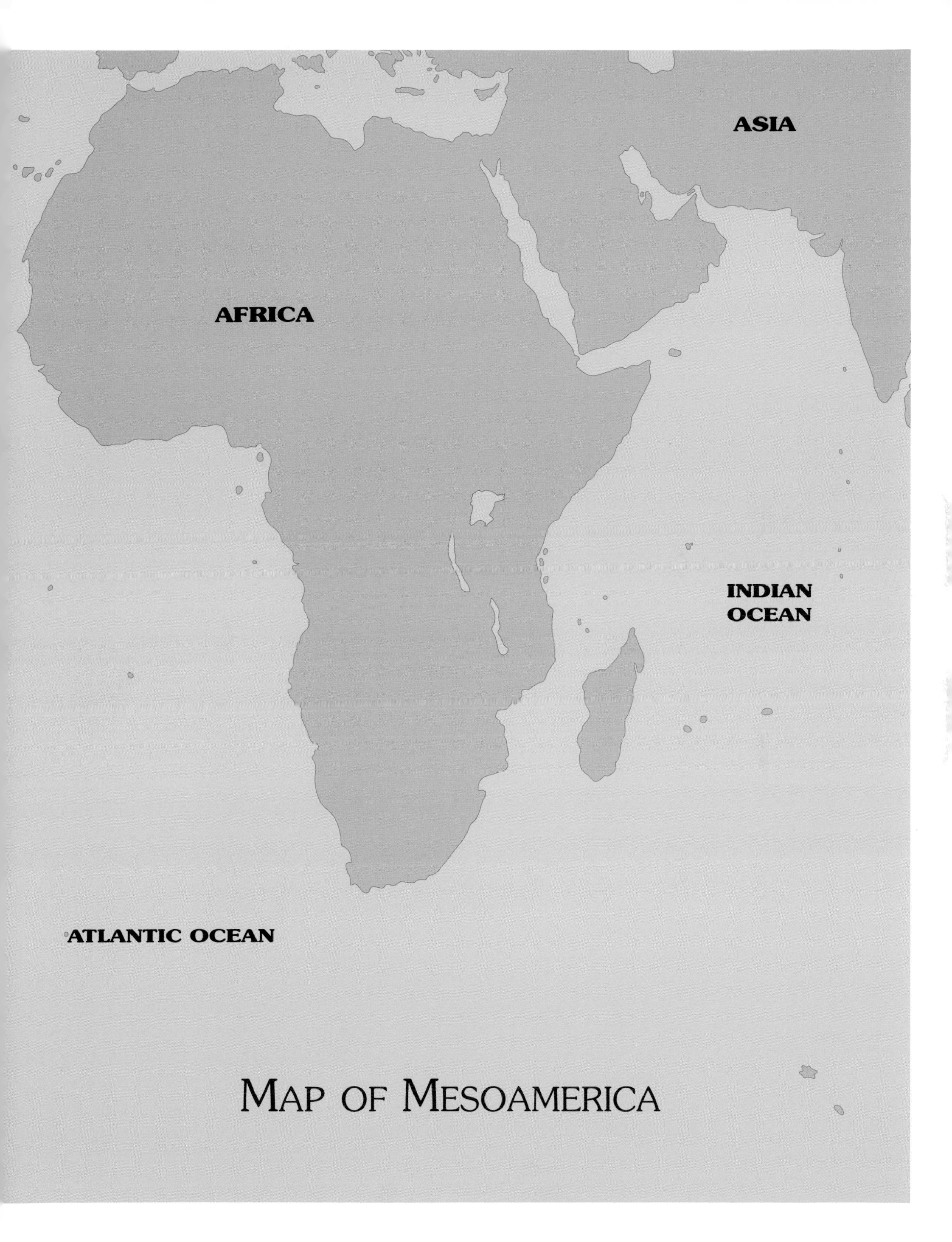

MAP OF MESOAMERICA

Glossary

Afterlife
The idea that life carries on after death.

Alliance
Where people/groups/nations cooperate for a specific purpose.

Atlatl
A wooden spear thrower.

Aztec
Mesoamerican people who lived in northern and central Mexico.

Ball court
Large open courtyard where the Mesoamerican ball game was played.

Beheading
A killing where the head is cut off.

Bloodletting
The practice of cutting human flesh to release blood as a gift to the gods.

Cannibalism
The eating of human flesh by another human being.

Chacmool
A stone statue used as a tray.

Chilan
The main priest in the world of the Maya.

City-state
A state that is based around an independent city.

Civilization
An advanced state of human society, where there is a high level of culture, science, industry, and government.

Deities
A person or being that is seen as a god or goddess or a divine character.

Inca
A civilization based in western South America.

Incense
Material that is burned to produce sweet-smelling smoke during religious ceremonies.

Legend
A story about mythical or supernatural beings such as the gods.

Maya
Mesoamerican people who lived in southern Mexico and Guatemala.

Mesoamerica
The area from central Mexico south to the border of Costa Rica.

Obsidian
A dark, glassy volcanic rock that is formed from hardened lava.

Prophet
A person who speaks for god or a deity.

Pyramid
A large building that is square at the bottom and rises to a point.

Rite
A part of a traditional ceremony.

Ritual
A part of a religious ceremony.

Sacrifice
Ritual killing of people or animals to please the gods.

Slave
Someone who is forced to work for no pay and has no rights. They are often held against their will.

Slingshot
A length of cord used to throw missiles such as stones.

Toltecs
Mesoamerican people who lived in and near the central Mexican city of Tula.

Trepanation
The practice of drilling a hole in the skull.

Tribute
A gift collected by a ruler, a bit like taxes today.

Underworld
A place where dead souls go. It is often feared as the place of darkness and despair.

Warrior
A trained soldier.

The Aztec Calendar—The Xiuhpohualli

	Name of Month (and meaning)	Gods and Rituals
1	Atlacacauallo (ceasing of water)	Tlaloc, Chachihutlicue Children sacrificed to water gods
2	Tlacaxipehualiztli (flaying of men)	Xipe-Totec Gladiatorial sacrifice; dances by priests wearing the flayed skin of victims
3	Tozoztontli (little vigil)	Coatlicue, Tlaloc Flayed skins buried, child sacrifices
4	Hueytozoztli (great vigil)	Centeotl, Chicomecacoatl Blessing of new corn; maiden sacrificed
5	Toxcatl (dryness)	Tezcatlipoca, Huitzilopochtli Impersonators of these major gods sacrificed
6	Etzalcualiztli (meal of maize and beans)	Tlaloques Impersonators of water deities sacrificed by drowning; ritual bathing and dances
7	Tecuilhuitontli (small feast of the lords)	Huixtocihuatl, Xochipilli Impersonators of the gods sacrificed; ceremony of salt workers
8	Hueytecuihutli (great feast of the lords)	Xilonen Feast for goddess of young corn, lords offer gifts and feast for commoners
9	Tlaxochimaco (birth of flowers)	Huizilopochtli All the gods festooned with garlands; feasting on cornmeal cakes and turkey
10	Xocotlhuetzin (fall of fruit) Hueymiccaihuitl (great feast of the dead)	Xiuhtecuhtli Ceremonial pole climbing competition Sacrifice to fire gods by roasting victims alive
11	Ochpaniztli (sweeping of the roads)	Tlazolteotl Sweeping of house and roads; mock combat
12	Teoleco (return of the gods)	Tezcatlipoca Ceremonies welcoming gods returning to earth; sacrifices by fire
13	Tepeihuitl (feast of the hills)	Tlaloc Ceremonies for mountain rain gods; human sacrifices and ceremonial cannibalism
14	Quecholli (precious feather)	Mixcoatl-Camaxtli Ritualistic hunt following fast; sacrifice of game and ceremonial feasting
15	Panquetzaliztli (raising of the banner)	Huitzilopochtli Homes and fruit trees decorated with paper banners; race procession; massive sacrifices
16	Atemoztli (water decends)	Tlaloc Festival honoring water gods; children and slaves sacrificed
17	Tititl (stretching)	Llamatecuhtli Sympathetic magic to bring rain; women beaten with straw-filled bags to make them cry
18	Izcalli (resuscitation)	Xiuhtecuhtli Image of god made from amaranth dough; feasting on tamales stuffed with greens
	Nemontemi (empty days)	Five unlucky days; no rituals, general fasting

Find Out More

Books

Baquedano, Elizabeth, and Barry Clarke. *Aztec, Inca, and Maya* (DK Eyewitness Books). New York: DK Children, 2005.

Philips, Charles. *Everyday Life of the Aztec and Maya*. London: Anness Publishing, 2007.

Powell, Julian. *Gruesome Truth about the Aztecs*. London: Wayland, 2008.

Websites

Ancient American Art
www.carlos.emory.edu/ancient-american-art

Library of Congress
www.loc.gov/exhibits/earlyamericas/online/precontact/

Mesoamerican Sites and Cultures
www.mnsu.edu/emuseum/prehistory/latinamerica/meso/mesotable.html

About the Author

Sean Callery is a children's writer and teacher. He writes on a wide range of subjects including history, science, and the environment. He is also the author of *The Gem Guide to Dictactors*, the history section of the *Kingfisher Explore Encyclopedia*, and he contributed to *The Encyclopedia of Dinosaurs and other Prehistoric Animals*.

Index

Page numbers in *italics* refer to illustrations